Jabari Jabari
What I love about me...!

Written By
Amber Hill

illustrated By
Ananta Mohanta

Jabari Jabari! What I Love About Me...?

Copyright © 2022 by Amber R. Hill. All rights reserved.

No parts of this book may be produced or utilized in any form or by any means, electronic or mechanical, including photocopying, recording, or by any information storage or retrieval, without written permission from the publisher. For permission request, contact the publisher at the email address below.

Epiphany-Hill Publishing
An Imprint of Epiphany-Hill Enterprises, LLC
Website: www.epiphanyhillenterprises.com
Email: epiphanyhillenterprises@gmail.com
Printed in The United States of America

ISBN: Paperback 978-1-7370549-3-1
ISBN: Hardcover 978-1-7370549-4-8

Dedication Page

This book is dedicated to my amazing son Jabari Hill and the amazing young learners in our world. Always remember you were made from greatness and born to shine! Continue to let your light shine bright!

Jabari Jabari what do you love about you? Daddy Daddy I love ...

My hair that is loc'd full of velvet ropes

My carmel face that is oval shaped
My eyes that are round and droopy for me to see

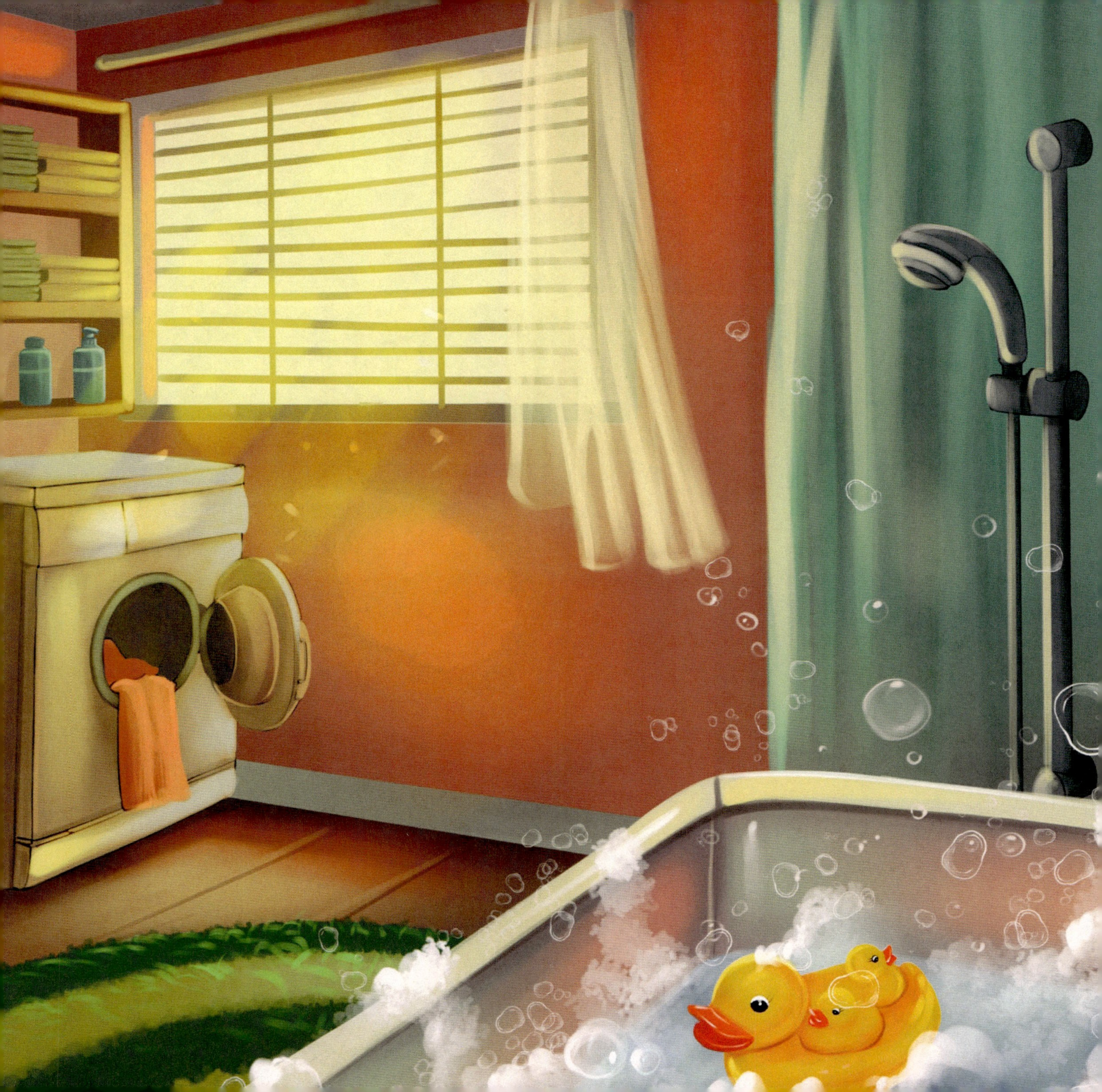

My carmel wide nose that helps me smell things

My full lips that connect to my mouth for me to speak

My cheeks that are soft and sometimes messy

and my narrow ears
that helps me hear

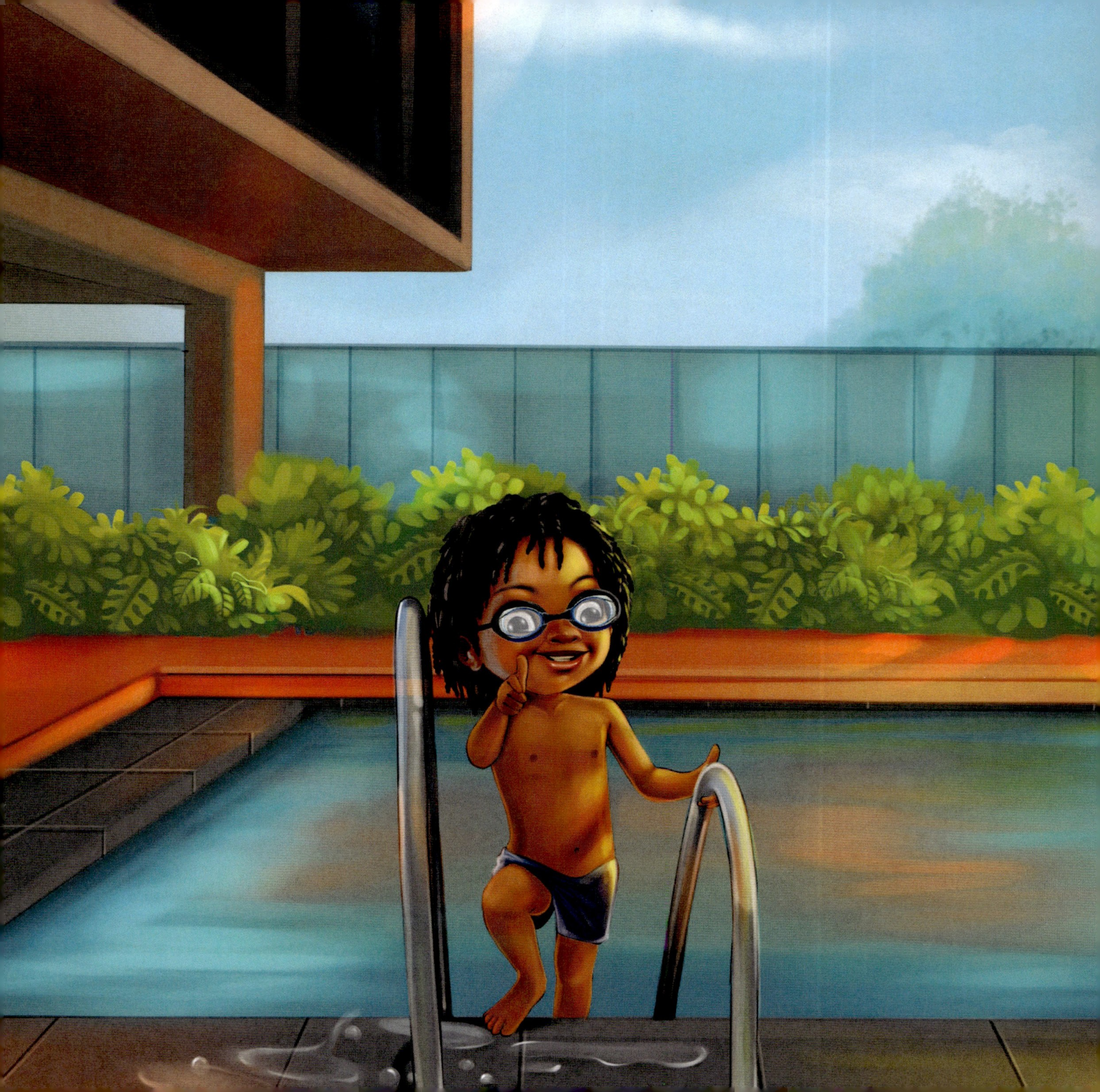

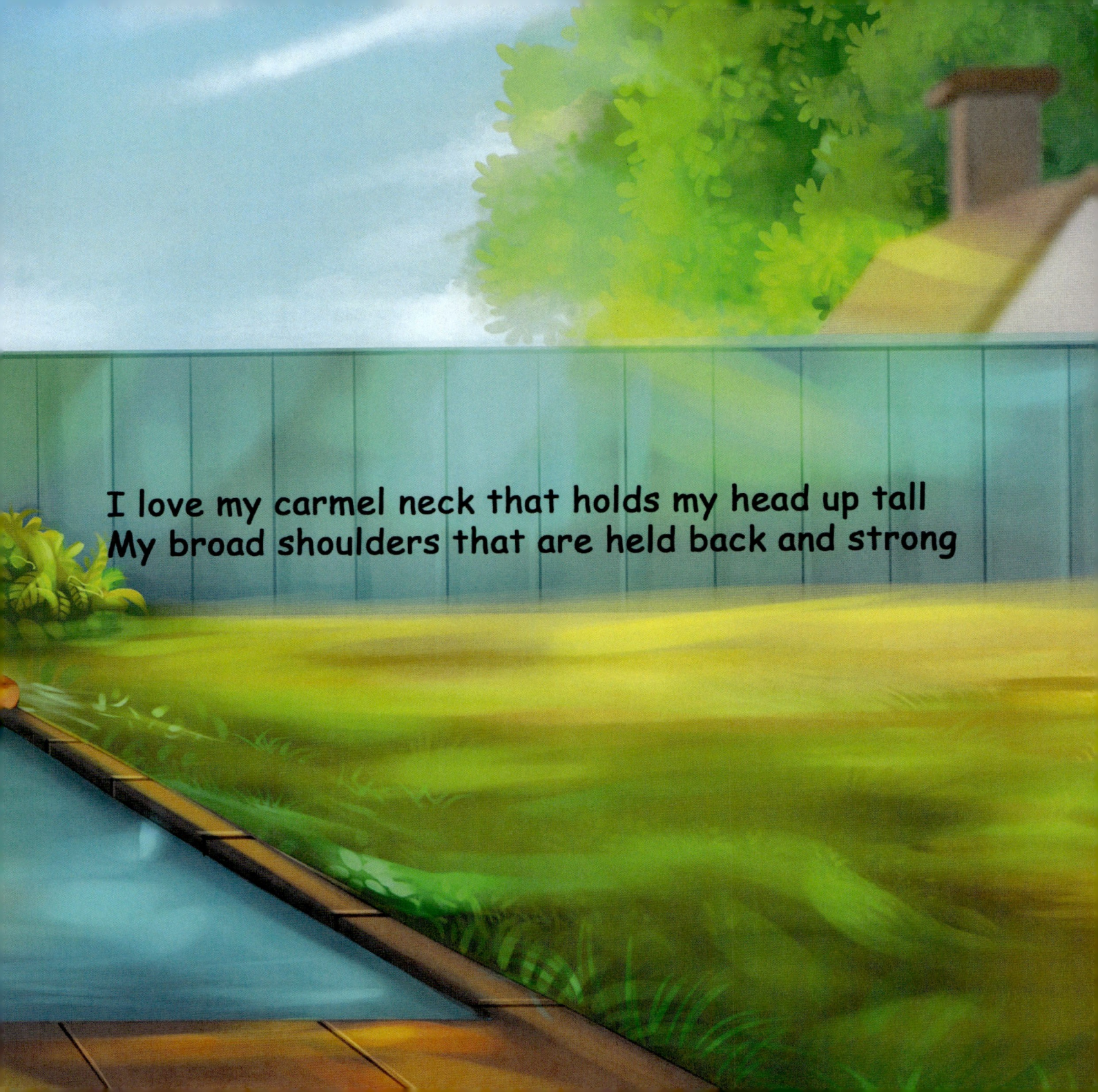

I love my carmel neck that holds my head up tall
My broad shoulders that are held back and strong

My arms that I can wave to and from

My elbows that are hard and sometimes bends

My tiny fingers that helps me touch and feel

My soft stomach that loves to be tickled here

and my wrists that turns and moves my hands

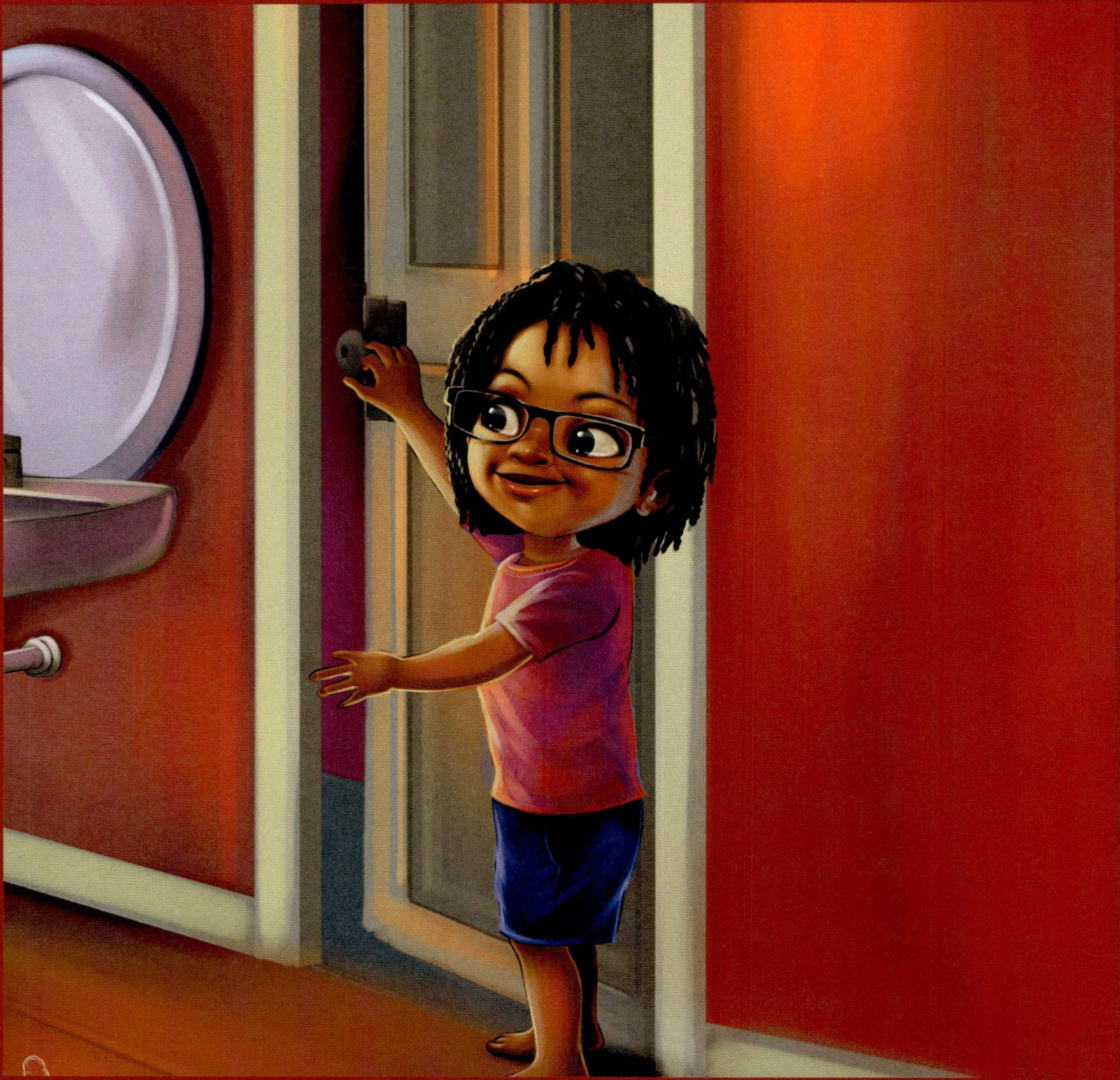

I love my waist
that is above my hips

My hips that I can move just like this

My legs that are big and long

My knees that helps me bend down small

My ankles that helps me twists my feet.

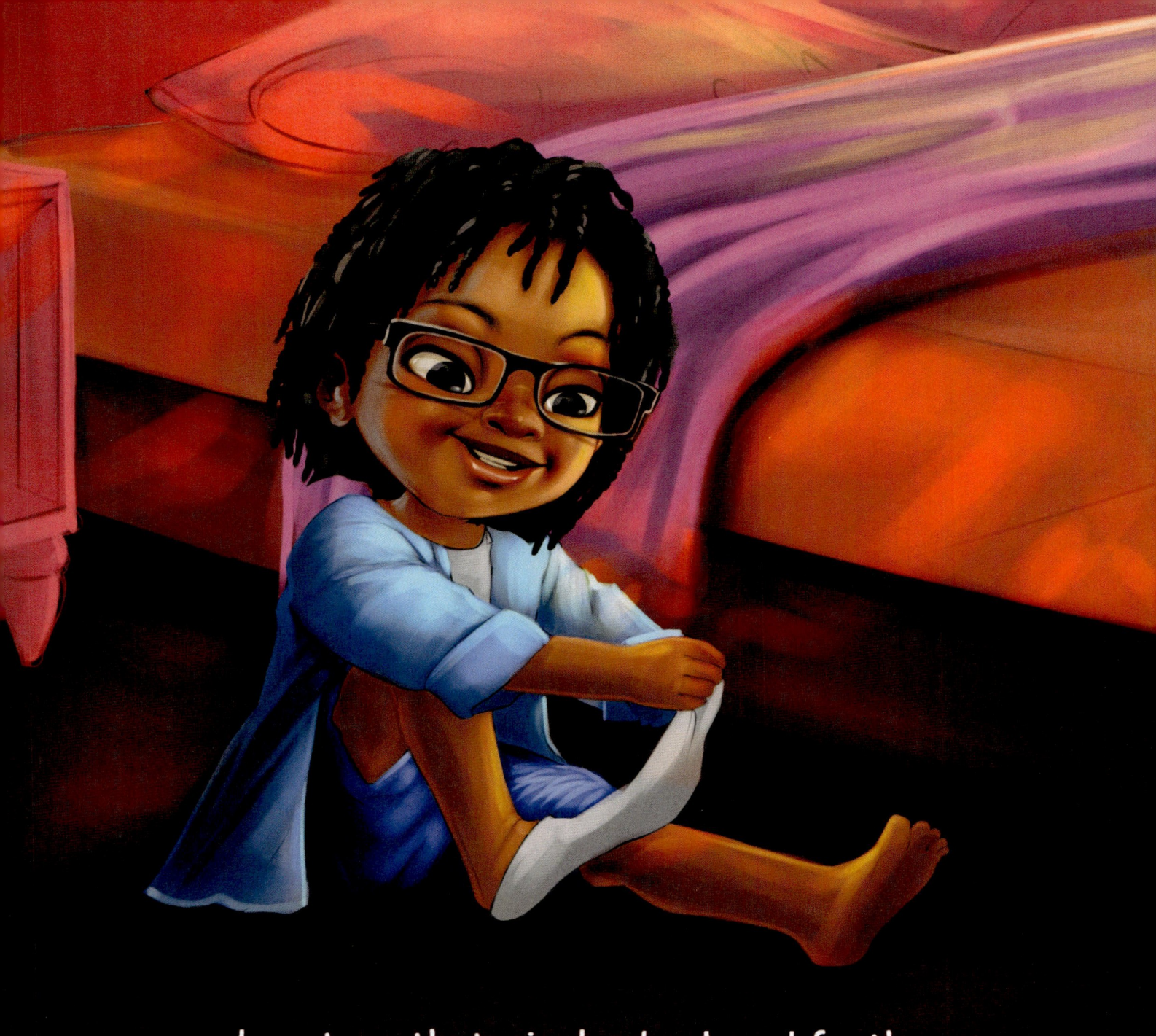

and my toes that wiggles back and forth

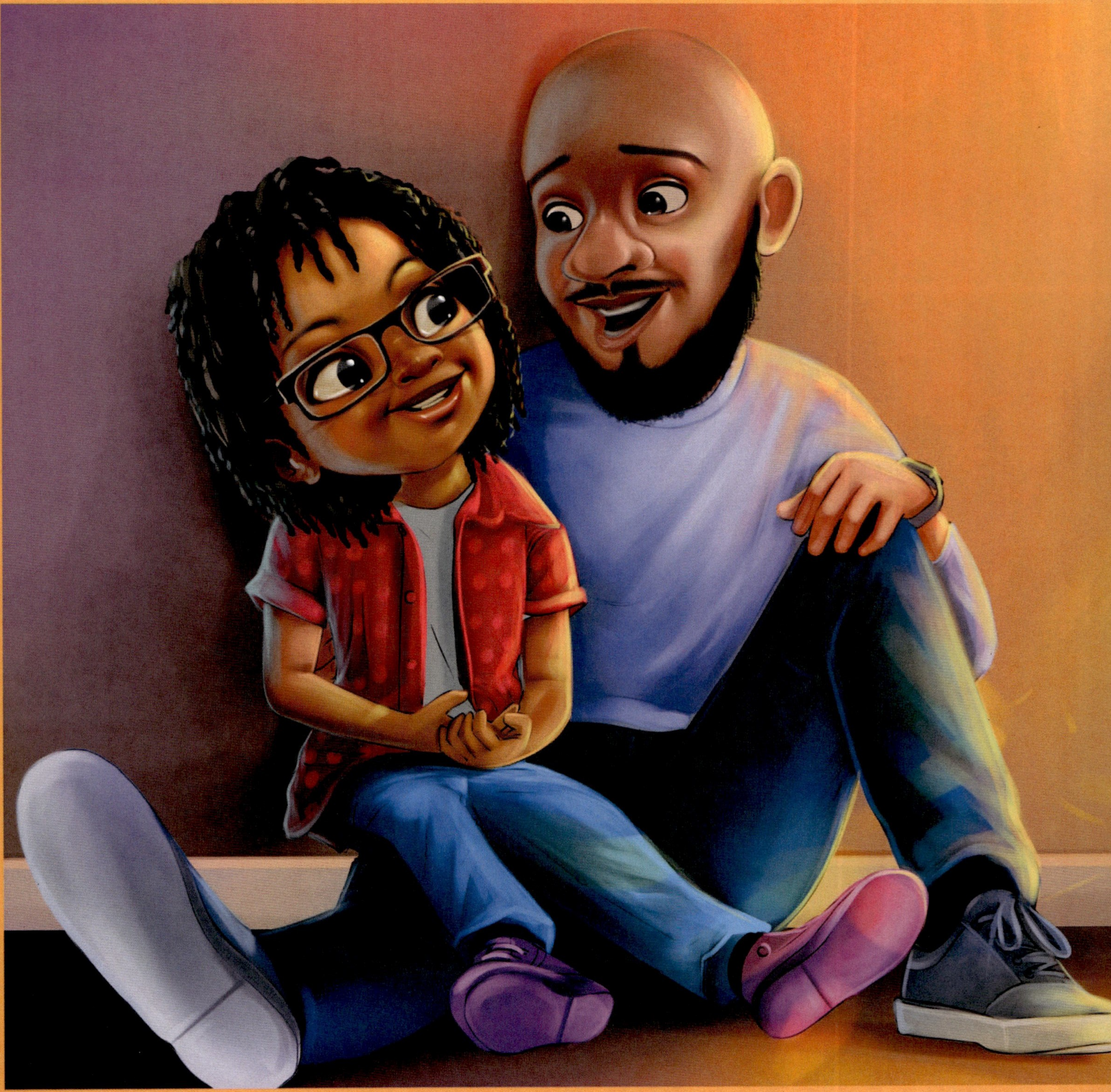

But most importantly Daddy, what I love about me is I am an image of you which makes me happy!

Special Thanks to...

The love of my life: my husband, James, and my beautiful sons: Jayden, Jabez, Jabari, and Jacobi; I am truly blessed to have amazing men in my life that always love me, support me in my endeavors, and encourage me to be great! You are the best family a woman can ask for!

I want to thank God for continuing to allow me to write and publish books for our youngest learners. God, you continue to give me the grace and strength to endure all things throughout this adventure. Thank You! Proverbs 31:25: "Strength and honor are her clothing; She shall rejoice in time to come."

I am also very grateful for my parents: Tasco and Dianne Williams. My siblings Tasco Williams, Candace Jones, Marie Williams, Sparkle Williams, and Brianna Williams. My In-loves, James and Geraldine Hill. And my extended family and friends. I appreciate your constant support and encouragement throughout this journey! I love you all!

Lastly, I thank my Illustrator, Ananta Mohanta, for bringing out my visions into beautiful art. You did a fantastic job! I am thankful for our collaboration.